If you were me and lived in...

Colonial America

Carole P. Roman

Illustrated by Sarah Wright

With accompanying illustrations by Kelsea Wierenga

For Zachary- you astonish me.

Book Design by Kelsea Wierenga

Copyright © 2016 Carole P. Roman

ISBN: 1523234075

ISBN 13: 978-1523234073

CreateSpace Independent Publishing Platform, North Charleston, SC

If you were me and lived in...

Colonial
AMERICA

If you were me and lived in Colonial America, you would have been born in London, England, almost 400 years ago in about 1620. This is what the city of London looks like today.

This is the England you would have left to come to the New World. What do you see as the biggest challenges?

If you were a boy, your parents might have called you Comfort or Abraham. They may have chosen Patience or Mercy for your sisters' names. What do the names tell you about the society?

Your parents may have chosen to follow the new Protestant religion.

In the early 1500s, England was a Catholic (Cath-o-lik) country. Henry VIII was king, and he had one daughter with his wife, Queen Catherine. He wanted to assure the succession with a male child, but his wife was getting too old to have more children. He fell in love with Anne Boleyn (Bo-lyn) and tried to divorce his wife. The Catholic Church in Rome refused to let the divorce happen, so Henry broke away from the church, creating a new national church called the Church of England. He declared himself the head of his new church and changed some of the ways people worshiped. His daughter, Queen Elizabeth I, continued with the new faith.

Many people had already embraced this new religion and were called Reformers or Protestants. They wanted a simpler church and thought that Henry and Elizabeth didn't change it enough. They thought the church should be plainer, and the prayer books needed to be in their own language. They demanded that some of the rituals be eliminated. These people were called Puritans. They called for the formation of a new church and were known as Separatists.

What do you think the name Separatists tells you about them?

In England in the 1600s, it was illegal to be part of any other church than the ruler's. Queen Elizabeth had died, and her cousin James Stewart became king. While he was a Protestant, many felt he wasn't strict enough, and they complained. The church reformers presented him with a list of things they wanted to be abolished. King James the First wanted to keep things the way they were with Elizabeth, the old queen. He thought he was being tolerant of everybody. The Protestants were offended when he refused to embrace their ideas and felt persecuted. Many fled to the Dutch Netherlands where they could practice the way they desired.

Your parents might have lived for a year or two in the Dutch Netherlands, but despite finally being able to practice their religion, they had to learn a new language. It was hard for them to find work, and they did not want you to join the Dutch army. In 1620, they heard of a couple of ships that were sailing to a new place to settle in a land without persecution. They were traveling to a land where colonies of people like them were able to settle in homes and worship the way they wanted. These ships were called The Mayflower and The Speedwell.

The ships set sail together in September, 1620, and leaks caused The Speedwell to return to Europe.

The Mayflower made landfall in the deep winter after a sixty-six-day journey.

The ship was originally supposed to land near the Hudson River in New York, but dangerous shoals and bad weather forced the ship in a northerly direction]to New England. The settlers named the place where the ship finally arrived Plymouth.

The people decided to form a new government to keep order. They needed a contract for all the settlers to follow to keep peace and ensure they would survive in the harsh new land. They wrote up a set of laws for them all to live by. All the men were called upon to agree with the rules. Your father signed the Mayflower Compact, which set up the colony's government.

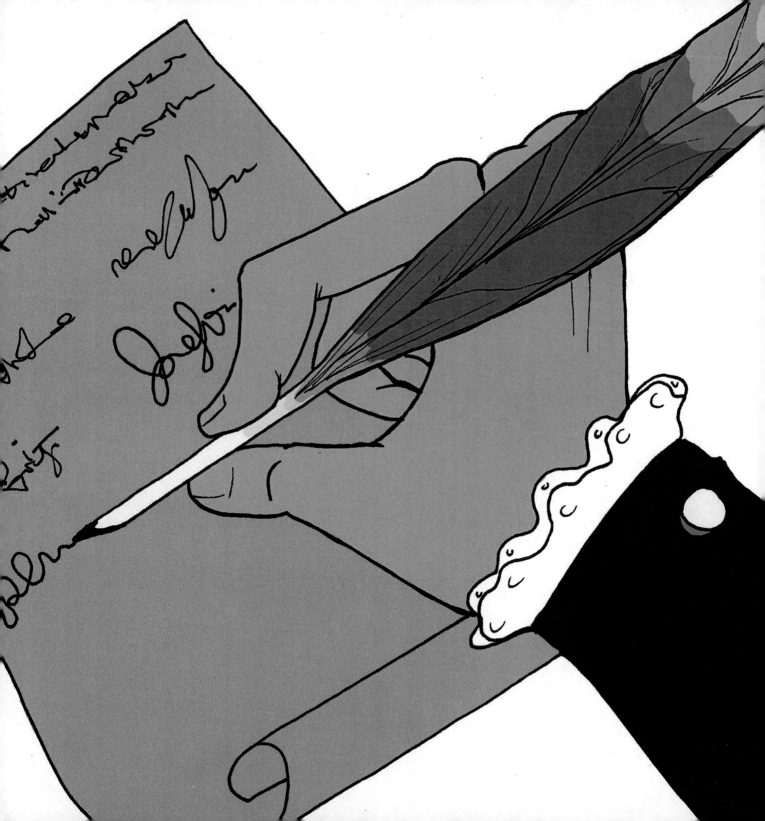

Your father and uncle scouted to find a good place to set up camp. After a few weeks of searching, they found an abandoned Native American village. There was a good harbor, ample water supply, and fields to be used for planting, all on a hill that made defending the community easier.

December was cold that year. You had a nasty head cold, and while you were not feeling well, others were much worse. A graveyard was created for many who could not survive the bitter weather and lack of permanent housing. Imagine arriving after a long journey to a land gripped in winter; the landscape was as forbidding as the moon with its snow-covered, frozen earth and not a dwelling in sight. There were no streetlights, stores, or church as well as no conveniences or friends, only raw land and the limited supplies brought from Europe. Everything had to be made from scratch.

Your father brought tools, nails, and iron hardware. Every day, he and your uncle went into the woods and used axes to chop down trees. First they built a frame, like a skeleton of the house. Then they bundled reeds from the marshes to make thatched roofs similar to those in England.

22

Outside, they created clapboards or shingles to cover the exterior walls of the home. Inside, they took dirt, clay, and grass to make a sort of plaster they called "daub" (dawb).

They reinforced it with interlaced rods and sticks called "wattle" (wat-tel) to make the interior walls of the house. It could take two months to finish a home; you had to live exposed to the cold winter winds for most of that first winter.

The home your father and uncle constructed was not large compared to the cottage you left behind in Europe; it seemed primitive. It had one room with a dirt floor. Everything from cooking to working or sleeping was done in this communal room. You had little or no privacy, which sometimes led to fierce fights with your little sister.

Your mother cooked in a fireplace that, once lit, always contained a fire. It took up most of the wall. It had a chimney that removed some of the smoke out of the room. Inside, the house was dimly lit, and the smells of all the people, food, and candles made it stuffy. It was drafty when the cold wind blew through spaces in the walls. You constantly had to plug the holes with mud. There was one small window with a shutter that barely covered the opening. Your uncle slept in the loft, which was a storage space built onto the wall above the ground floor. He had a ladder to climb up, and you envied the space. At least, he had a piece of the cabin for himself. Mama kept the dried food and herbs up there, so it smelled better than the rest of the cabin. She grew those herbs and some vegetables in a small garden outside the door that she and your sister tended.

By the end of the first winter, your father was proud to say that they had built eleven homes for the colonists. You now lived in a village! The town elders called it something different. They explained that since farming was the major role of their new home, they decided to call their town a plantation.

If you never saw another lobster again, it would be too soon. You were so tired of the creepy creatures. The sea was crawling with them. What you wouldn't do for a nice mutton stew or pasty (pas-tee) made from a bird cooked in rich gravy!

Everybody knew that bread, beer, and any kind of meat were what made Englishmen healthy. The problem was the only food you ate was what was available in this new land. The first three years were brutal, as far as food was concerned. Your father struggled to grow crops in the unfamiliar and temperamental climate. It was backbreaking work of clearing land, planting seeds, and waiting for that first harvest. Fruits and vegetables were foraged in the summer. Your family brought the wrong kind of fish hooks, and the only thing you caught in the beginning were those dreadful lobsters. You waited patiently for supplies, but it took years for ships to come with things from home. You forgot about supplies like sugar and butter. You didn't remember what they tasted like!

You made friends with a native boy. You met him at the river one day. You were scared, but he was friendly and somehow you learned to talk to each other by using hand movements. He was your age, and when he stopped laughing at your clumsy fish hook, he taught you how to hunt and trap the local game. He came from the Wampanoag (Wam-pan-nog) tribe, and he had skin that was much darker than yours. He had long, straight black hair. He gave you seeds of the strange corn that grew in abundance in his village. He showed you how to cut a small piece of herring or fish to include in the furrow when you planted the large kernels of corn. The fish made the land fertile.

When the corn crops were finally harvested, there were many delicious things to do with the sweet kernels. You helped your mother pull them off the cob and dry them over the fire. Your sister and you pounded the red, yellow, and black kernels into a flour that made a delicious bread and filling porridge. You ate it at every meal. Your native friend helped you plant beans, squash, pumpkins, barley, and melons. He taught you to save the largest seeds for planting the next spring. This made sure you grew bigger and better crops with each harvest. By the time chickens, goats, sheep, and cows arrived on the ships the following spring, your table groaned with the rabbits, turkeys, ducks, and geese you had learned to trap. Oil, sugar, salt, and vinegar had to be imported from England. It was expensive and necessary to preserve the food that arrived via the ships.

The one thing your family missed most was beer. You were reduced to drinking dangerous water and somehow survived. It was healthier than drinking milk, your mother said.

You would start your day with a "break fast," eating bread, butter, cheese, and, if you were lucky, some dried meat.

Dinner came in the afternoon and was the biggest meal of the day. You would start with porridge and bread made from the sweet corn. There was always meat and fowl, probably in a thick stew.

Supper was something you grabbed in the early evening after all the chores were done. Nothing was wasted, so you probably finished whatever leftovers you had from dinner.

In the fall of 1621, the colonists celebrated both their survival and harvest with a three-day celebration. Massasoit (Mas-sa-soit), the native chief, and some of his tribe joined you for a feast to show gratitude for survival. It was the first Thanksgiving. In March of 1621, your father and some of the elders signed a treaty with the chieftain, making rules for the two societies to live side by side. If anyone stole anything, it would be returned, and the person was sent to their people for punishment. Weapons would be left behind when they met. They would act as allies in times of war, supporting each other. The two groups would not harm each other and lived in harmony. You were happy for the native boy's friendship.

You were proud to point out that by 1627 the colony had grown to 160 people. Soon you had extra vegetables, and you were able to trade them with the natives for fur. The inbound ships from Europe wanted fur. Back home, people trimmed clothing with it and made hats from the beaver skins. Your father sold the fur to a merchant on the ship, and soon there was extra money for all the little things you had missed so dearly.

You owned two fine shirts that your mother made for you during the winter. You wore an old close-fitted doublet (dub-let) that belonged to your father. It was a thick jacket with long sleeves, padded shoulders, and big horn buttons down the front. You wished they would let you wear a leather jerkin (jer-kin), like your uncle, but your mother said it wasn't warm enough. It was soft leather vest that made movement easier when you worked. You had a pair of baggy knee-length breeches (bree-chez) and thick woolen stockings held up with black ribbon garters at the knees. The outfit was all in dark colors, and you had to be careful to make your clothes last. Your shoes were too big; your mother bought them in Europe in anticipation that you would grow into them. You wore a large felt hat with pride. It was a lot better than the gown they made you wear until you were five years old. It was the happiest day of your life when they "breeched" (bree-ch-ed) you, allowing you to wear trousers like the men did.

43

Your mother and sister wore a long white shift made from cotton that looked like the night rails they wore at bedtime. They had petticoats (pet-tee-coats) tied around their waists under their skirts that went down to their ankles. Their dresses were divided into two parts: the bodice (bod-is) and skirt. The bodice was tight-fitted and buttoned down the front of their upper torso. Sleeves were separate and had to be attached to the bodice. They wore pretty hand-made lace collars and cuffs. Your mother always wore a white apron. Her skirt barely touched the floor. Mama pulled her hair tightly off her face and wore it under a cap.

45

Thirty-two children made the trip over on The Mayflower to settle in the country with their parents. Their lives were filled with daily chores. Small children were expected to tend the chickens, fetch water, and, as they got older, help in the field. Girls had to work with their mothers, mending, cooking, and caring for younger siblings.

You were busy tending to the family cow, fishing, and helping with trapping meat. Your sister knew how to preserve food, sew, and could cook as well as your mother. She wasn't even twelve years old yet!

Your parents let you play the occasional game of leap-frog, marbles, and a "crosses and naughts," but you noticed your sister gave her poppet (pop-it) away to the first baby born in the colony. You guessed she was too old for the doll. The baby was a boy named Peregrine (Per-er-grine). You wondered what a boy was going to do with a poppet.

Most schooling was arranged in the home. You attended a "petty" (pet-tee) school and learned basic math and reading. You used a paddle made from an animal horn for your lessons. Papa cleaned it and attached a leather belt so you could sling it over your shoulder. He glued a page from the Bible for you to memorize on the front. You carved designs in the horn and were proud of how it looked. Papa spent the early evening reading the Bible to the whole family. You knew most of it by heart. Mama taught both you and your sister how to read and write, but only in the winter after the harvest was finished.

So you see, if you were me, how life in Colonial America could really be.

Here are some people who influenced the colonies on the entire eastern seaboard.

Ann Hutchinson (1591-1643) was a Puritan and mother of 15 who rebelled against the Massachusetts Bay Colony. She was tried and thrown out of the colony. She resettled in nothern New York.

Peter Minuit (1580-1638) was Director of the Dutch colony of New Netherland. Minuit is acknowledged as the person who arranged the purchase of Manhattan Island for the Dutch from the Native Americans called the Lenape, which later became the city of New Amsterdam and after the British took over, New York.

William Penn (1644-1718) was an English businessman, philosopher, early Quaker, and founder of Pennsylvania. He helped develop the city of Philadelphia.

Pocahontas (1595-1617) was a Native American associated with the colonial settlement at Jamestown, Virginia. She was said to have protected Captain Smith when her father wanted to kill him. Some say this story is not true.

Captain John Smith (1580-1631) was an English soldier, explorer, and author. He was considered to have played an important part in the establishment of Jamestown, the first permanant English settlement in North America. He was a leader of the Virginia Colony.

Myles Standish (1584-1656) was an English military officer hired by the Pilgrims for the Plymouth Colony. Standish played an important role in defending the colony. He was elected the first commander and continued to be re-elected for the remainder of his life.

Glossary

Abraham (Aye-bra-ham)- a popular boy's name in Colonial America.

allies (al-lies)- a common motive or purpose uniting two or more people, nations, or countries together.

Anne Boleyn (Bo-lyn)- Henry VIII's second wife and the mother of Elizabeth I. Henry broke from the Catholic Church so he could divorce his first wife and marry her.

bodice (bod-is)- a woman's vestlike garment, similar to a corset.

break fast (break-fast)- to break the fast in the morning and eat the first meal.

breeched (bree-ched)- when a boy is finally allowed to stop wearing gowns and moved to pants.

breeches (bree-chez)- pants that end just below the knee.

Catholic (Cath-o-lik)- belonging to the Catholic Church or Church of Rome.

Church of England (Church of Ing-land)- the church created by Henry VIII when the Catholic Church wouldn't let him divorce his first wife.

clapboards (clap-boards)- long, thin boards used to cover walls and roofs of buildings.

colonial (co-lo-nee-ul)- the period of American history from the 17th century to 1776, under the rule of Great Britain, France, and Spain.

colonists (col-uh-nists)- the settlers who came to the New World.

communal (com-mun-al)- living and sharing everything in one place.

Comfort (Com-fort)- a popular boy's name in Colonial America.

corn (corn)- a hearty type of corn.

cottage (cott-age)- a small home.

crosses and naughts (kross-es and nawt-s)- the American version is the game "tic-tac-toe."

daub (dawb)- plaster, clay, or another substance used for coating a surface, especially when mixed with straw to form a wall.

divorce (di-vorce)- to end a marriage.

doublet (dub-let)- a man's short close-fitting padded jacket, commonly worn from the 14th to the 17th century.

Dutch Netherlands (Duch Neth-er-lands)- the Kingdom of the Netherlands. It was a small, densely populated country located in Western Europe.

elders (eld-ers)- the oldest and most respected members of a community.

felt (felt)- a nonwoven fabric.

fertile (fur-tle)- capable of growing crops and plants.

forage (for-ije)- search widely for food or provisions in the wilderness.

fowl (foul)- chicken, duck, or geese.

garters (gar-ters)- thin bands of fabric fastened about the leg, used to keep up stockings and sometimes socks.

Henry VIII- King of England (1509-1547) (Hen-ree)- Henry VIII is known for his role in the separation of the Church of England from the Roman Catholic Church.

horn (hawrn)- an animal horn used for buttons and tools.

Hudson River (Hud-son River)- the river that flows from north to south through eastern New York.

James I- King of England (1603-1625) (Jay-mz)- Many Protestants felt persecuted by his religious beliefs.

jerkin (jer-kin)- a long leather vest.

leap-frog (leep-frog)- a game of hopping over the bended form of the child standing in front.

lobsters (lob-sters)- shellfish with long bodies and meaty tails, which live in crevices on the sea floor.

loft (lawft)- an upper story or attic in a building, directly under the roof.

Massasoit (Mas-sa-soit) (1581–1661)- the leader of the Wampanoag tribe in the 1600s.

Mayflower Compact (May-flou-er Com-pact)- the first governing document of the Plymouth Colony. It was written by Separatists who fled persecution in Europe. Later they were referred to as Pilgrims.

mending (mend-ing)- sewing, usually to repair a tear in clothing.

Mercy (Mer-cee)- a popular girl's name in Colonial America.

mutton (mut-ton)- meat of domestic sheep.

native (ney-tive)- a person who lives where he was born.

Native Americans (Ney-tive Ah-mer-ah-cans)- the people who lived in North America before the settlers came.

New England-Connecticut, (Noo Ing-land-Con-nect-ee-cut)- a northeasterly region of the U.S. comprising the states of Maine, Vermont, New Hampshire, Massachusetts, Connecticut, and Rhode Island.

New York (Noo - York)- originally a Dutch settlement called New Amsterdam; it was purchased from a group of natives called the Lenape. It later became New York City when the British took over.

night rails (nite-rales)- nightgowns.

paddle (pad-el)- a flat wooden and horn board used in school for children as a notebook in Colonial times.

pasty (pas-tee)- a hearty mix of meat and vegetables cooked in a flaky crust.

Patience (Pay-shents)- a popular girl's name in Colonial America.

Peregrine (Per-er-grine)- a popular boys's name in Colonial America.

persecution (per-see-cu-shun)- hostility and ill-treatment due to race political or religious beliefs.

petticoats (pet-tee-coats)- an undergarment worn underneath skirts.

petty (pet-tee)- a school for boys in Colonial America.

plantation (plan-tat-shun)- a large piece of land where crops are planted for commercial sale.

Plymouth (Plim-uh-th)- a town in Massachusetts established by the Pilgrims in 1620.

poppet (pop-it)- a doll.

porridge (por-ridge)- a dish made by boiling ground, crushed, or chopped grains in water or milk and served hot in a bowl.

preserve (pre-serve)- prepare (fruit, vegetables, etc.) by cooking or smoking with sugar or pickling, for long-term storage without spoiling.

primitive (prim-ee-tiv)- outdated or dating back to an earlier time.

Protestant (Pro-tes-tant)- a person who has protested the belief of the Catholic Church and changed the doctrine to suit his religious needs.

Puritans (Pure-it-tains)- a group of English Protestants in the 16th and 17th centuries who sought to purify the Church of England from all Roman Catholic practices, maintaining that the Church of England was only partially reformed.

Queen Catherine of Aragon (Cath-er-in of Ar-a-gon)- Queen of England from 1509-1533 and the first wife of King Henry VIII.

Queen Elizabeth I (E-liz-a-beth I)- Queen of England and Ireland from 1558-1603.

reeds (ree-ds)- a common name for several tall, grass-like plants that were bundled and used for thatched roofs.

reformers (ri-form-ers)- the individuals who brought about the Protestant Reformation of the sixteenth century.

rituals (rit-u-als)- practices and ceremonies.

Separatists (Sep-par-et-tists)- those who sought to separate from the accepted beliefs of the church at the time.

settlers (set-lers)- people who came to North America to settle and farm the land.

shift (shift)- a simple kind of undergarment like a slip.

shingles (shin-gals)- thin pieces of wood that are overlapped and put on a house or roof.

shoals (shohls)- sandbanks.

shutter (shut-er)- a cover for a window that can be opened and shut.

siblings (sib-lings)- brothers and sisters.

The Mayflower (The May-flower)- one of the ships that transported the first English Separatists, known today as the Pilgrims, from Plymouth to the New World in 1620.

The Speedwell (The Speed-wel)- the second of the two ships that planned the journey to the New World, but constant leaks caused it to return to Europe.

succession (suc-ces-shun)- the action or process of inheriting a title, office, property, etc.

Thanksgiving (Thanks-giv-ing)- the day of giving thanks for the blessing of the harvest from the preceding year.

thatched (tha-ched)- bundled reeds used for roofs.

tolerant (tol-er-ant)- showing a willingness to accept others even if they didn't agree with them.

vinegar (vin-a-gar)- a sour liquid, made from wine or cider, to pickle food.

Wampanoag (Wam-pan-nog)- one of the native peoples that lived in North America.

wattle (wat-tel)- the material for making fences, walls, etc., consisting of rods or stakes interlaced with twigs or branches.

Please visit my blog for additional resources for this book and others, including printable worksheets, coloring pages, topics for essays, and critical thinking.

caroleproman.blogspot.com

32557088R00038

Made in the USA
Middletown, DE
08 June 2016